Sassy Soap

THIRTY-FIVE PROJECTS
TO GET YOU IN A LATHER

Sassy

Soap

THIRTY-FIVE PROJECTS TO GET YOU IN A LATHER

FAITH SUGARMAN

Photography by Michael Hnatov

STERLING PUBLISHING CO., INC.
NEW YORK

Edited by Ana Deboo
Photographed by Michael Hnatov
Designed by Kay Shuckhart/Blond on Pond

Library of Congress Cataloging-in-Publication Data

10 9 8 7 6 5 4 3 2 1

Sugarman, Faith.
Sassy soaps : thirty-five projects to get you in a lather / Faith
Sugarman ; photography by Michael Hnatov.
p. cm.
Includes index.
ISBN 0-8069-1539-0
1. Soap. I. Title.
TP991 .S84 2004
668'.12--dc22

2003024146

Published by Sterling Publishing Co., Inc.
387 Park Avenue South, New York, NY 10016
© 2004 by Faith Sugarman
Distributed in Canada by Sterling Publishing
C/o Canadian Manda Group, One Atlantic Avenue, Suite 105
Toronto, Ontario, Canada M6K 3E7
Distributed in Great Britain by Chrysalis Books Group PLC
The Chrysalis Building, Bramley Road, London W10 6SP, England
Distributed in Australia by Capricorn Link (Australia) Pty. Ltd.
P.O. Box 704, Windsor, NSW 2756, Australia

Sterling ISBN 0-8069-1539-0

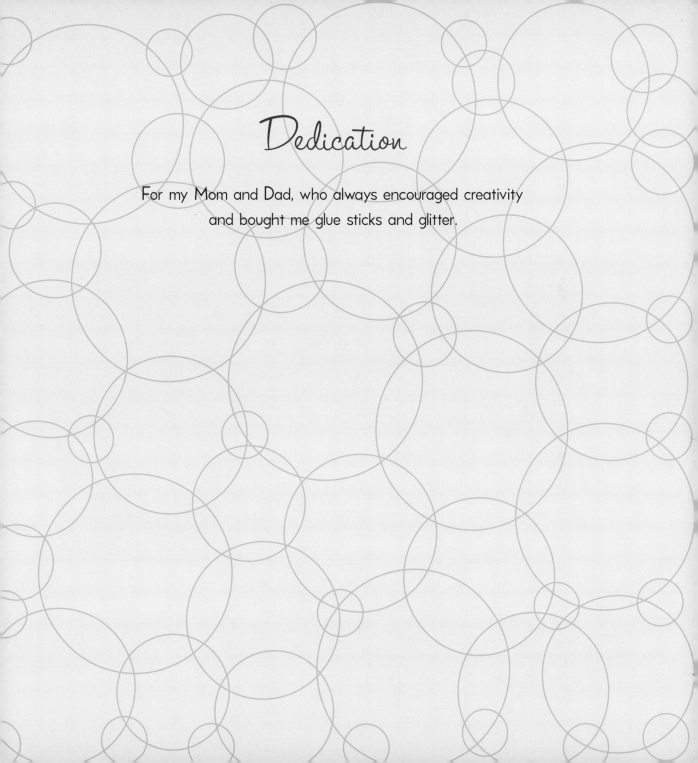

Dedication

For my Mom and Dad, who always encouraged creativity
and bought me glue sticks and glitter.

Contents

CHAPTER 3

CHAPTER 4

CHAPTER 5

CHAPTER 6

CHAPTER 7

"What is elegance? Soap and water!"

—Cecil Beaton, 1959

Introduction

Smooth, fragrant, and luxurious—a great bar of soap is so satisfying. You've seen all those cool bars in gift and bath shops. You've probably bought quite a few for your friends and yourself. But maybe you didn't know that you could whip up nifty soap at home.

Didn't you think it was more complicated than that? You may have memories of learning about traditional soapmaking in school or on a visit to someplace like Colonial Williamsburg. That kind of soapmaking requires that you work with such unpleasant ingredients as fat or the caustic substance lye. Also, you'd have to wait for the soap to cure before you could use it.

All of those complicated steps have been eliminated for melt-and-pour soapmaking. Just melt down store-bought glycerin soap bricks and pour them into molds to create new soaps. Pop the soap out of the mold and you're ready to take a bath with it immediately!

It's inexpensive, easy, and fun—and nearly every project in this book can be completed in less than two hours.

You'll learn the basics, as well as more advanced techniques like making your own latex molds from scratch. We'll review everything, from embedding toys to creating loaf soaps and making weird and wonderful themed novelty bars. And this is just the beginning. Once you're familiar with the materials and techniques, the sky's the limit!

Go forth and make soap.

Getting it Together: Supplies and Materials

Soapmaking is a pretty simple matter, really. A little soap base and a mold are the minimum requirements. Of course, there's a lot of territory to explore beyond the pure white, oblong bar. You can get as fancy or funky as you want. You can get into ever more elaborate molds. Fragrances, additives, colors—added either singly or in combi-nation—contribute even more. The choices are all yours. Here is some information to help you get started with those decisions.

Soap Bases

Premade melt-and-pour soap base is available in both white (opaque) and clear and can be found at most craft stores and hobby shops. It's usually sold in one- to five-pound blocks. It resembles a brick and is usually either shrink-wrapped or packaged in hard plastic.

Soapmaking is increasing in popularity, so it's getting easier to find precolored soap base, as well as specialty soap bases like avocado and cucumber, goat's milk, coconut oil, and oatmeal. Instructions in this book all call for white or clear soap base—but don't hesitate to substitute one of these varieties if you'd like to.

Of course, if you're unable to find the supplies you want locally, there's always the Internet, where you can shop for anything and everything 24/7. Online sources may be your best bet if you need large quantities of soap base. Many vendors sell it in bulk, either in brick form or in forty- to fifty-pound tubs. That's a lot of soap—but it's probably an economical way to go if you plan to split the order between a few fellow soapmakers.

You'll find that the prices for melt-and-pour soap base vary greatly. Avoid very inexpensive choices; they may be of poor quality and loaded with fillers such as wax and chemical additives.

Sassy Soap

HOW MUCH SOAP DO YOU NEED FOR A PROJECT?

Since each project in this book is different, it's hard to say exactly how much soap you'll need for each scenario. A "standard" size bar takes three to five ounces of soap. Anything under three ounces qualifies as small and would be best suited for hand soap. Anything larger than six ounces would be oversized—a bar much bigger than that is too cumbersome to be functional.

Except in the final chapter on novelty soaps, approximate soap amounts are included for each project. In some cases, though, you'll have to exercise your own judgment—your mold may not be exactly the same as the one used for a particular project.

The good news is that, even if you overestimate, leftover melt-and-pour soap base doesn't go to waste. It can be melted down a second or even a third time for another project.

Molds

There are many types of craft molds on the market, and lots of them are designed specifically for soapmaking. Chances are you want at least a few heavyweight plastic or rubber molds in plain bar shapes or rounds of various sizes. After all, you can do a lot of interesting projects with those tried-and-true forms—and traditionally shaped bars are hard to beat for a satisfying experience in the bath.

But when you're ready to experiment with other shapes, there is no end to the alternative types of molds you can use. In fact, once you know the secrets of latex mold making, there's almost nothing three-dimensional that you couldn't turn into a soap mold!

SOAP MOLDS AND CRAFT MOLDS

This type of heat-tolerant mold is readily available in plastic and occasionally in rubber as well. It is an excellent choice, because it can withstand the high temperature of the melted soap, and it's very easy to remove the finished product from the mold. These come in plain and ornate designs. And since the popularity of melt-and-pour soap has increased dramatically, commercial moldmakers have responded accordingly. The shelves of most craft and hobby shops carry a good assortment.

GELATIN MOLDS

Gelatin molds are a lot of fun to use because they often come in fun shapes and designs, some of them specific to holidays and special occasions. They're great for making festive guest soaps.

Sassy Soap

ICE CUBE TRAYS

Novelty ice cube trays can be found at supermarkets and discount stores. These are made of rubber and have designs like fruit, dolphins, and hearts. If cutesy isn't your thing, take a look at flea markets or online auctions for more eclectic and unusual ice trays.

PLASTIC FOOD STORAGE CONTAINERS

Small square or rectangular food storage containers are the ideal size for making individual bars of soap. The larger ones can be used to make loaf soaps. Be sure to use medium-weight plastic containers, as opposed to the disposable variety, which are too flimsy to tolerate high temperatures.

Also, remember to keep your stash of soapmaking containers separate from the ones you use to store food.

MAKESHIFT AND FOUND MOLDS

Keep your eyes open and let your creativity flow. Some examples of makeshift molds include plastic canisters, sandbox toys, plastic applesauce cups, cookie and cracker trays, and yogurt containers—basically, anything that can tolerate having hot soap poured into it is fair game. If a makeshift mold seems too lightweight or weak, it probably is. Stick with heavier-duty plastics.

CANDY MOLDS

Candy molds are fabulous for making unusual and novelty soaps. They come in an astonishing variety and can be found at party and kitchen supply stores. Of course, the best selection will be available from candy- and chocolate-making supply shops.

The only problem is that candy molds are often made of lightweight plastic that isn't intended to withstand the high temperatures of melted soap base—but don't despair! Buy as many candy molds as you want.

You can use the candy molds to create durable homemade molds with liquid latex, which is available at any hobby shop. These molds will be good for hundreds of bars of soap..

HOMEMADE RUBBER LATEX MOLDS

Latex molds are perhaps the best choice for working with melt-and-pour soap, especially once you move into making novelty soaps. Latex can withstand the temperature of hot soap, and it's flexible, so it's easy to remove the soap from the mold. Another benefit is that it's incredibly sturdy and long-lasting.

It's really quite easy to make your own molds, although it does take a bit of time. Once you know how, a whole world opens up for you. There's really no object you can't convert into a bar of soap. If you can imagine it, you can make it a reality.

Here's how:

Sassy Soap

SUPPLIES:
THE OBJECT TO BE MADE INTO A MOLD
An old CD or other nonporous flat object, to create a border
around the opening of the mold
Double-sided tape for attaching CD
Safety glasses
Rubber gloves (optional)
Brush-on liquid latex rubber
(available at craft and hobby shops)
Small paintbrush
Jar of water

The first step is to choose the object you want to work with. The object must have a smooth, nonporous surface. For example, you can make a rubber latex mold of a plastic candy mold. Or look for interesting objects around the house. The best candidates for mold-making are in one piece and fairly symmetrical. For this project I found a cool looking acrylic cube—actually, the bottom piece of a photograph holder. It's just the right size and shape for a small bar of soap.

Attach the object to an old CD or other nonporous flat object with double-sided tape. This will create a border around the opening of the mold.

Choose a well-ventilated area to work in and, before getting started, put on the safety glasses. This is important because latex contains ammonia, which can be dangerous if it comes in contact with the eyes and lungs. You might also want to use rubber gloves.

Using the paintbrush, apply a thin coat of latex rubber to the prepared object and over a 2-inch area on the CD all around the edge of the object. Allow the latex to dry (this will take about two hours). Be sure to keep the paint-brush in the jar of water or wash it thoroughly after applying each coat. Otherwise, the latex will dry on the brush and ruin it.

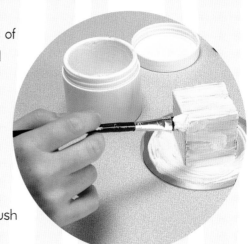

Once the first coat has dried, repeat the process until there are ten to fifteen coats of latex compound coating the object. The mold is thick enough when the rubber is completely opaque. The latex will have taken on a yellowish tinge.

Once the final coat has had several hours to dry, gently pull the edges of the rubber mold upward toward you. As long as you've painted the latex onto a nonporous object and base, the mold should come loose very easily.

Sassy Soap

 Ta-da! You now have a perfect inverse replica of the object that you painted.

Colorants, Pigments, and Micas

COLOR TABS

These little tablets of solid color are added directly to the soap when it is being melted. Follow the manufacturer's directions as to how much colorant to use.

LIQUID CONCENTRATES

Concentrates provide crisp, clear colors and can be blended to create unique shades. These liquids are a popular choice because the colors tend not to fade or bleed into each other in soap projects.

FOOD COLORING

Food coloring isn't the best option for melt-and-pour soap, although many hobbyists use it anyway. Over time, the soap may fade or develop dots of color. Don't opt for food coloring if you're going to sell your products at a crafts fair—this isn't an FDA-approved method for tinting for soap.

WATER-BASED POWDERED COLORANT

Many people who make "bath bombs" use this form of colorant, and it can be used in melt-and-pour soap, too. It is a little harder to find and more expensive than other colorants. But just a touch of this powder goes a long way.

COSMETIC-GRADE PIGMENTS

These natural, cosmetic-grade oxides are intended to be used in soaps and cosmetics.

COSMETIC-GRADE GLITTER

You'll find a variety of colors and shimmers available. I like the iridescent cosmetic glitter best. Always use cosmetic-grade glitter, never standard craft glitter—that can cause skin irritation and damage to the eyes.

Sassy Soap

SOAP LORE: From 1712 to 1853, soap was heavily taxed as a luxury item in England. (In fact, to make sure soapmakers didn't cheat and sell their wares on the black market, tax collectors came by to lock up the soap-making equipment at night.) It wasn't until society became more conscious of the importance of hygiene in fighting disease that Parliament repealed the tax, making soap accessible to greater numbers of people than ever before.

MICAS

Micas come in either the pearlescent or the sparkly variety. When you add them to clear soap base, you get a cloudy, dreamy effect.

Fragrances

In many ancient civilizations, fragrance was important. Certain scents took on cultural and religious significance. That may not always be the case nowadays, but scent still has a very powerful influence on us.

There are so many wonderful fragrances available that it's sometimes hard to choose which one to use! Some are valued for their aromatherapeutic properties, while others just smell fabulous. Fragrances can help reflect the mood of the soap as well as your personal preferences.

FRAGRANCES AND THEIR TYPES

FLORAL	FRUITY	SENSUAL/EARTHY	CRUNCHY	UNIQUE
Iris	Mango	Jasmine	Grass	Tomato
Leaf	Lemon	Patchouli	Milk & Honey	Green Tea
Rose	Mixed Fruit	Musk	Cucumber	Lemongrass
Gardenia	Apple	Sandalwood	Rain	
Echinacea	Watermelon	White Ginger	Ocean	
Freesia	Raspberry	Chocolate	Sunflower	
Hyacinth	Peach	Bay Rum	Eucalyptus	
Heather	Strawberry	Aloe Vera		
Violet	Kiwi	Oatmeal		
Lily of				
the Valley	Apricot	Wheatgerm		
Magnolia	Cranberry			
Tulip				

Sassy
Soap

FRAGRANCE OILS

Fragrance oils are synthetically produced, so they embody a wide range, from traditional florals and fruits to perfumes, food scents, exotic blends, and beyond. Fragrance oils come in a variety of grades. Be sure to only buy cosmetic-grade oils that are intended for use in soap and cosmetics. Your local crafts shop probably has a small selection of soap-safe fragrance oils, but for a wider range, try soapmaking supply sites on the Internet, as well as specialty mail order catalogs.

ESSENTIAL OILS

Essential oils are made from the concentrated essences of herbs, flowers, trees, and other vegetation. They tend to be considerably higher in price than fragrance oils. However, many soapmakers swear by them for their superior, all-natural fragrance.

It is important to remember that essential oils are concentrated and should be used very sparingly. A good rule of thumb is to use one drop per bar of soap and no more than one teaspoon per pound of melt-and-pour soap base.

FRAGRANCE COCKTAILS

Why limit yourself to just a single fragrance when you can concoct a terrific new scent by mixing fragrances? To help decide on your recipe, cut an index card into strips and use a dropper to dab a tiny amount of each fragrance oil you want to blend onto a separate strip

TRY THESE MIX-'N'-MATCH COMBINATIONS

Chocolate + Coconut
= Candy Bar

Plumeria + Vanilla
= Hawaiian Sunset

Rosemary + Mint
= Summer Herb Garden

Hazelnut + Vanilla = Coffee Shop

Apple + Cinnamon
= Apple Strudel

Eucalyptus + Peppermint
= Invigorating

Tangerine + Lime = Fruit Candy

Chocolate + Peanut Butter
= Peanut Butter Cups

Vanilla + Orange = Creamsicle

Sassy Soap

(as if you are testing perfumes). Smelling the strips in combination will give you a general idea of what your finished product will be like.

Additives

Additives can be anything from finely ground oatmeal to herbs to certain types of flower petals. Many soapmakers enjoy working with them.

Some of these elements are believed to be therapeutic; others are purely decorative or fragrant; and some are used as exfoliants. It is important to note that, with additives, a little bit goes a long way. (You'll use approximately one tablespoon per pound of soap.) They will usually affect the clarity, consistency, and color of your soap.

Some types of soap, such as the handmilled varieties, can be made with fresh fruits and vegetables because benzoin is added to the soap as a preservative. You can't use fresh additives with melt-and-pour projects—your soaps will get moldy and rancid. Stick with powdered or dried additives.

Also, keep in mind that not all herbs or flowers are appropriate for use in soap. A plant may be natural, but it can still cause allergies and other skin irritations. It's best to work with the ones that are known to be safe for this purpose, such as those sold in the soap section of your local crafts shop or on soap supply websites.

A FEW COMMONLY USED ADDITIVES

TO CREATE MORE LATHER:
Whole-milk powder or goat's milk powder

TO SOFTEN THE SKIN:
Buttermilk powder

TO SOOTHE THE SKIN:
Apple fiber

TO ADD VIBRANT COLOR:
Calendula petals

TO COMBAT OILY SKIN:
French clay

TO EXFOLIATE NATURALLY:
(1 tablespoon per pound of soap)
Apricot meal
Cornmeal
Powdered loofah
Poppy seeds
Strawberry seeds
Cranberry seeds
Finely ground oatmeal

Objects for Embedding

People—especially kids—love soaps with objects embedded in them. Those are some of the most popular soaps sold at gift stores. And, as you'll learn in Chapter 4, you can make them too!

Toys that are appropriate for embedding are everywhere. Toy stores, dollar stores, closeout shops, your child's castoffs, stationery stores, party stores—even garage sales. Just be sure to use only objects made of PVC or soft rubber with smooth, rounded edges. Hard, brittle plastic toys can have jagged edges that may scrape the skin or damage the eyes. It's also best to stick with toys that are made of only one piece. They're less likely to break into smaller bits as the soap is used.

Avoid toys that are too small, like mini-erasers. They may look pretty inside the soap at first,

but they'll fall off as the bar wears down— and they won't be nearly as attractive clogging the drain. Not to mention that they're a choking hazard for young children. (Always label soap with an embedded toy as being a potential choking hazard for children under the age of three.)

Before You Dive In:

How to Make
Melt-and-Pour Soap

Nearly every project in the book follows pretty much the same pattern. Once you've

mastered these basic steps—and it won't take long—you're ready to begin thinking

up your very own melt-and-pour projects!

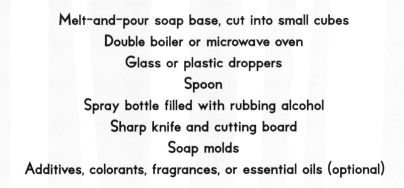

Melt-and-pour soap base, cut into small cubes
Double boiler or microwave oven
Glass or plastic droppers
Spoon
Spray bottle filled with rubbing alcohol
Sharp knife and cutting board
Soap molds
Additives, colorants, fragrances, or essential oils (optional)

The Basic Method, Step-by-Step

STEP ONE: MELT IT DOWN

A. THE DOUBLE BOILER METHOD

A double boiler is the best way to melt soap base on the stovetop. Simply fill the bottom portion of the pan with water (not so much that it reaches the bottom of the insert, though) and place the soap base in the inner pan. Don't have a double boiler? Improvise! Set a metal bowl over a pot of simmering water.

The purpose of the double boiler is to use steam heat to melt the soap base—it isn't quite as hot as the boiling water, so the soap can't overheat and boil, which could result in moisture loss and a crumbly finished product.

Keep the burner on low heat as the soap base dissolves into liquid form. When it is melted down, remove the pan from the heat source and stir the soap gently. Allow the soap to cool for about three to five minutes before pouring it into the mold.

Sassy
Soap

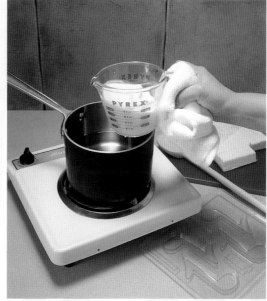

TOP LEFT: Cut soap into small cubes.

TOP RIGHT: Place soap base in boiler.

LEFT: Keep burner on low heat as soap base dissolves.

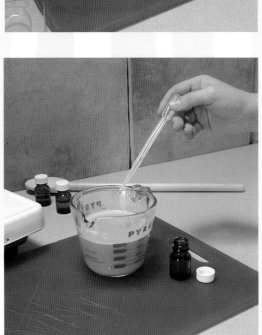

TOP LEFT: Add colorants and fragrances.

TOP RIGHT: Stir gently for a few seconds.

LEFT: Add additives a drop at a time.

B. THE MICROWAVE METHOD

Many people prefer to simplify the melting process by putting the soap base in the microwave. It's a quick, easy alternative to the double boiler, and cleanup is minimal. Plus, you can heat the soap in increments, which offers you greater control.

Using a heat-safe glass container, microwave the soap cubes on medium power for about thirty seconds. If there are still some solid pieces, continue to heat the soap at ten-second intervals until it is melted. Protecting your hands with pot holders, remove the container from the microwave, stir the melted soap until it is smooth, and allow it to cool for about three minutes before pouring the soap into the molds.

STEP TWO: ADD COLOR, SCENT, AND OTHER ADDITIVES

If you are planning on using them, add colorants, fragrances, or additives to the melted soap after it has had time to cool for three minutes or so. Stir the mix gently for a few seconds.

> SOAP LORE: Perhaps the earliest example of transparent glycerin soap was developed by the Cornishman Andrew Pears after he opened a cosmetics shop in London in 1789. Pears, who started out as a barber, set out to create a soap that could be marketed as a beauty aid. Regular soaps of the day could be quite harsh. His bar was gentle—and gorgeously translucent. Pears soap is still popular two centuries later.

Sassy
Soap

STEP THREE: POUR THE SOAP INTO THE MOLD

Pour the soap into the mold. You may notice a few small air bubbles on the surface. Those can be eliminated with a quick spritz of rubbing alcohol from a spray bottle. Try to do this as quickly as possible, before your soap begins to harden.

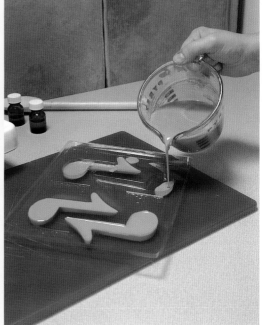

STEP FOUR: COOL THE BAR UNTIL IT'S HARDENED

The cooling process will depend upon how large the bar is. A good rule of thumb is to let it sit in the mold for at least forty-five minutes to an hour.

Once the soap has hardened, push gently on the back of the mold. The soap should release easily—it's soap, after all; it's slippery! However, if you're having trouble getting soap out of a plastic mold, try running cool water over the outside of the mold, then gently push the soap out. Many soapmakers suggest putting the mold in the freezer for a short while, but I've found that over time this can cause plastic molds to weaken and crack.

Since melt-and-pour soap base does not contain lye, there is no "curing" time needed. Feel free to lather up with it any time.

TEMPERATURE IS EVERYTHING

One thing you'll learn quickly is that temperature is crucial when it comes to working with melt-and-pour soap. This is especially true when you're embedding toys into bars of soap and making loaf soaps. If the soap is too hot, the object won't set properly. If you try to embed soap shapes within a bar or loaf and the melted soap you're pouring in is too hot, the soap shapes will melt and the colors will bleed. Embedded toys could either sink or float to the top.

There is no "right" way to determine the exact timing that should be used. Always allowing hot soap to cool for a few minutes before pouring it will greatly diminish many temperature-related problems. Mostly, though, timing and temperature are a matter of trial and error. You'll get the hang of it.

STEP FIVE: WRAP IT!

If you don't plan to use your new bar of soap immediately, wrap it in plastic to prevent moisture loss. Melt-and-pour soap is glycerin-based, and leaving it exposed to the air can cause small beads of moisture (or "sweat") to form on the surface.

You can also use cellophane bags, which are more visually appealing, especially if the soap is going to be given as a gift. Decorate the bag with pretty ribbons, stickers, or whatever appeals to you. Looking for interesting ways to package your creations? Later in the book we'll go over some suggestions.

Safety Considerations

Kids love soapmaking, but make sure there's adult supervision. Children shouldn't heat or pour the soap themselves. Instead, have them help with planning the design and choosing and mixing in colorant, fragrance, and additives.

Don't let the soap to come to a boil. This can make for a dry, crumbly bar.

When melting soap in the microwave, use microwave-safe glass containers only. Avoid plastic bowls, which may melt and cause spills. If hot soap does get on your skin, run the area under cool water and seek medical attention, if necessary.

If your soaps will be given as gifts or sold at craft fairs, be sure to label any that include fragrances or additives. Always mark soaps with embedded toys as potential choking hazards and indicate that they are intended for children ages three and up.

C H A P T E R   3

Getting Your Feet Wet:
Projects for Beginners

Let's start slow and easy. You can't just dive right in and create unique and wonderful projects before you have a basic understanding of what working with melt-and-pour soap is like. These four beginner-level projects will give you an idea of the steps that are involved and some the choices you can make. And the end results—simple as they may be—are pretty pleasing.

Wholesome Bowl of Oatmeal Soap

You know how you're supposed to begin the day with a hearty, wholesome breakfast? It's not a bad idea to get into soapmaking the same way. This satisfying starter project is about as easy as to make as heat-and-serve quick oatmeal.

YIELD: 1 BAR

1 teaspoon ground regular oatmeal (not instant)
3–5 ounces white soap base
1 very small plastic bowl
Fragrance or essential oil (optional)
Pinch of coarse-grained raw (Demerara) sugar, for garnish (optional)

1. Using a food chopper, blender, or food processor, grind the oatmeal until it is about the consistency of cornmeal—take care not to make it too powdery.

2. In a double boiler over low heat, or using the microwave at medium power, melt down the white soap base; then remove it from the heat and set it aside.

After the soap has been cooling for two or three minutes, slowly stir in the oatmeal.

 If desired, add fragrance. Many scents work well with this soap. Try oatmeal, milk, honey, or vanilla.

 Pour the soap into the small plastic bowl, top it with a very light sprinkling of the sugar, if you want to, and allow it to harden. Remove from bowl.

A soap bubble is the most beautiful thing, and the most exquisite, in nature ... I wonder how much it would take to buy a soap bubble, if there was only one in the world? One could buy a hatful of Koh-i-Noors with the same money, no doubt.

—Mark Twain, from *A Tramp Abroad*, 1880

NOTE: If the oatmeal ends up at the bottom of the bar, then the melted soap was poured into the mold while it was still too hot. No matter—just keep this in mind for next time. Even with the oats at the bottom, this will be a great, usable exfoliating bar.

The Personality Profile Color-Cube Bar

This one will add a little color to your repertoire. This cheerful bar (assuming you choose upbeat colors, of course—that will depend on whether you're having an up or down day, won't it?) will provide you with an intro to the embedding technique we'll explore more fully in Chapter 4. It will also give you a certain amount of insight into your personality. Do you go for loosey-goosey designs, or are you more a geometrical, checkerboard type? Do you like bright or wacky hues, or sensible earth tones?

YIELD: 1 BAR

2 ounces white soap base, cut
into small cubes and then divided into two
equal portions
2 shades of colorant (colors of your choice)
2 shallow plastic food storage containers
Spray bottle filled with rubbing alcohol
3 ounces clear soap base,
cut into small cubes
Plain soap mold, rectangular, oval, or round
Fragrance or essential oil (optional)

Sassy
Soap

In a double boiler over low heat, or using the microwave at medium power, melt down a portion of the white soap base; then remove it from the heat and set it aside. Slowly add the colorant of your choice. Allow the soap to cool slightly.

 Pour the colored, cooled soap into a plastic container and set it aside to harden.

 Repeat steps 1 and 2 with the remaining white soap base, using your second colorant this time.

 After the colored soaps have been hardening for at least fifteen minutes, gently remove them from their molds.

 Using a sharp knife, carefully cut the soap into small cubes and spritz them lightly with rubbing alcohol. This will prevent bubbles from forming on the surfaces of the cubes when you pour the clear soap over them.

6 Arrange the cubes in the soap mold according to your fancy and set the mold aside. Randomly jumbled cubes look great—or maybe you're more of an orderly checkerboard person.

7 Melt down the clear soap base and stir in fragrance, if desired. Set it aside to cool until a thin skin forms over the soap.

8 Pour the clear soap over the colored cubes in the mold. Don't worry if some of the cubes stick out above the level of the clear soap (this means you, obsessive checkerboard people)—that just adds character.

9 Allow the soap to harden for about forty minutes before popping it out of the mold.

VARIATIONS:

Instead of making colored cubes, you can use a melon-baller to create tiny colored spheres. If you do this, you might want to try using a round soap mold, too.

Try using tiny cookie cutters to make colored shapes to embed in the clear soap.

Sassy
Soap

42

Sculpted Swiss Cheese Soap

In this project you get to do a little sculpting—just to show you that the world of melt-and-pour soapmaking doesn't have to be all melting and pouring. If you've got a little Michelangelo hiding away inside you, soapmaking can help you let him out. Be careful not to make this one too realistic, though—a mouse might come along and spoil your handiwork by nibbling at it.

YIELD: 4 BARS

4 ounces opaque soap, cut
into small cubes
Yellow colorant
Fragrance or essential oil (optional)
1 large round soap mold
Paintbrushes, assorted sizes
Rubber mouse, for garnish (optional)

 In a double boiler over low heat, or using the microwave at medium power, melt down the soap base; then remove it from the heat.

 Add a few drops of yellow colorant and the fragrance, if you're using it. Stir well, then carefully pour the soap into the mold and allow it to harden for about forty minutes, then remove.

Using a large, sharp knife, cut the soap into quarters to make four wedge-shaped bars. Use the back ends of the various paintbrushes to make different-sized holes on the surface of the bars. Your goal is to create a Swiss cheese effect, and with a little practice this isn't difficult.

Garnish with a rubber mouse, if desired.

Sassy Soap

Cookie Cutter ABCs Soap

Wrapping up this chapter on the ABCs of soapmaking are these fun cutout letters. They're incredibly easy. (Who hasn't used a cookie cutter now and then? Or even if not, who'd have trouble learning?) They're also great for personalized projects, like spelling out a kid's name or creating a message for a compadre. Glitter makes a groovy addition to these bars, if you like a little sparkle in your day.

YIELD: 4 OR MORE BARS

1/2 pound opaque or clear soap, cut into small cubes
Colorant of your choice
Fragrance or essential oil (optional)
Cosmetic-grade glitter (optional)
Small, shallow heat-safe plastic tray
Assorted letter-shaped cookie cutters

 In a double boiler over low heat, or using the microwave at medium power, melt down the soap base; then remove it from the heat.

 Add a few drops of colorant—along with the fragrance and/or cosmetic glitter, if desired. Stir well, then pour the soap into the shallow tray and allow it to harden for about twenty-five minutes.

3 Carefully turn the soap out onto a flat surface, press the cookie cutters into the soap, and gently remove the letters.

4 Any soap that is left over can be remelted and made into more letters or saved for another project.

NOTE: You may want to make letters in more than one color. If so, melt the soap base and pour it into up to four different heat-safe containers. Stir a different colorant into each one and proceed as described above, taking care to choose correspondingly smaller molds to cool each color of soap in before cutting out the letters.

Sassy
Soap

Taking the Plunge: Soap with Embedded Objects

Both grown-ups and kids love soaps with cute or kitschy toys in them. You'll find plenty of soaps like this in high-end gift shops—but they're pricey. Why not make them yourself? For the cost of a single store-bought soap with a toy in it, you can make five or six bars.

There are two different approaches to making soap with toys inside: You can totally submerge the object in the bar—that works well with smaller toys. Or you can use the

partial-submersion method. That works best with larger rubber toys. The purpose is to make the toy seem to be floating or sitting on the soap. See Chapter 1 (page 13) for more hints on choosing the right toy for the job.

This chapter ends with two projects that involve embedding other pieces of soap in the bar instead of using toys. The process is very similar whether you're working with a toy or another piece of soap; both kinds of bar are spectacular—and the all-soap variety allows you to get just that much more washing done!

Sassy
Soap

Elephant in the Grass Bar

Y ou've heard of a snake in the grass, right? Well, a cheerful, pudgy elephant is cuter—and much less sneaky. Of course, you could make a sneaky snake-in-the-grass bar too, if you wanted. All you need is a little rubber snake!

YIELD: 1 BAR

2–3 ounces clear soap base, cut into small cubes
Green colorant
Fragrance or essential oil (optional)
PVC or rubber elephant toy
Round or square soap mold
Spray bottle filled with rubbing alcohol

 In a double boiler over low heat, or using the microwave at medium power, melt down the soap base; then remove it from the heat and set it aside to cool slightly.

 When a thin skin starts to form on top of the soap, add one drop colorant, as well as fragrance, if you'd like.

3 Squeeze the elephant toy gently and hold it under running water to draw a little bit of water in through the hole at the bottom of the toy. This will weigh it down so it won't float up and out of the melted soap base.

4 Pour the green soap base into the mold, filling it halfway. Spritz the toy lightly with rubbing alcohol. That will help the rubber surface adhere to the soap. Then simply drop the toy into the soap base, centering it as best you can. It may be necessary to hold the elephant by the head for a few minutes as the soap hardens around it.

5 Wait about one hour before carefully removing the soap from the mold.

Sassy Soap

Scrub-a-Dub Baby in a Tub Bar

This bar makes a terrific party favor for a baby shower. You can use almost any small plastic container for the tub, as long as it will hold the rubber baby. The one used for this project is actually from one of those single-serving packages of maple syrup!

YIELD: 1–2 BARS

2–5 ounces clear soap base,
cut into small cubes
Blue colorant
Fragrance or essential oil (optional)
1 or 2 small round or rectangular plastic containers to serve as "bathtubs"
1 or 2 small rubber baby squeaky toys
Spray bottle filled with rubbing alcohol

In a double boiler over low heat, or using the microwave at medium power, melt down the soap base; then remove it from the heat and set it aside to cool slightly.

 When a thin skin starts to form on top of the soap, add one drop colorant, as well as fragrance, if you'd like.

 Squeeze the baby toy gently and hold it under running water to draw a little bit of water in through the hole at the bottom of the toy. This will weigh it down so it won't float out of the melted soap base.

Pour the blue soap base into the plastic tub, filling it halfway. Spritz the toy lightly with rubbing alcohol, then drop the baby into the soap "bath," centering it as best you can. It may be necessary to hold the toy down for a few minutes as the soap hardens around it. The soap will be ready to handle after about one hour.

VARIATIONS

You might also want to try making:

 Duck-in-water soap

 Out-of-this-world soap: an alien toy embedded in clear soap base spiked with iridescent cosmetic glitter

 Pig-in-a-sty soap: a pig toy embedded in a brown "mud" base

Sassy Soap

52

Hospitable Hula Girl Guest Soap

Everyone likes a hula girl, whether for 1950s retro appeal or just sheer beachy fun. Post this lovely lady by the washroom sink to offer your houseguests a warm island welcome. Aloha!

YIELD: 1 BAR

3–4 ounces clear soap base,
cut into small cubes
Small rubber or PVC hula girl toy
Colorant of your choice
Cosmetic-grade glitter (optional)
Fragrance or essential oil (optional)
Soap mold of your choice
Spray bottle filled with rubbing alcohol

 In a double boiler over low heat, or using the microwave at medium power, melt down the soap base, then remove it from the heat. Add one or two drops colorant, as well as the glitter and the fragrance, if you're using them.

53

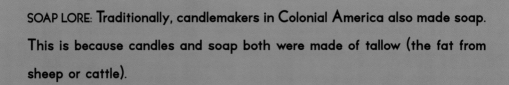

Set the melted soap aside and allow it to cool for a few minutes, until a thin skin forms on top. You want the toy to appear to be floating—it shouldn't sink to the bottom of the mold—so the temperature of the soap at this point is important. (This is really a matter of trial and error. And a bit of practice.)

Pour the soap into the mold. Then, very gently, press the toy all the way into the soap upside down (so she'll be face up when you unmold the bar). Spritz the top of the soap bar with rubbing alcohol once to prevent bubbles.

Allow the soap to harden for about an hour, then remove it from the mold.

Sassy Soap

Perfect Specimen Butterfly Bar

This is a great soap to give to natural history buffs or probably just about anyone. (Surely only a Scrooge doesn't like a butterfly!) It has a classic look. You'll find an assortment of pretty butterfly toys (and other bugs too, for that matter) at those nature- and education-oriented toy stores. Half the fun will be in choosing the toy to go inside!

YIELD: 1 BAR

4 ounces clear soap base, cut into small cubes
Fragrance or essential oil (optional)
Cosmetic-grade glitter (optional)
Colorant (optional)
Rubber or PVC butterfly
Soap mold of your choice
Spray bottle filled with rubbing alcohol

In a double boiler over low heat, or using the microwave at medium power, melt down the soap base, then remove it from the heat. If you'd like, add fragrance. Or try stirring in a pinch of glitter for a shimmery look. Or add a drop of colorant. (Or do all three!)

2 Set the melted soap aside and allow it to cool for a few minutes, until a thin skin forms on top. Your goal is to reach the correct temperature for floating the toy in the soap.

3 Pour the soap into the mold. Then, very gently, press the toy into the soap upside down (so it'll be face up when you unmold the bar). Spritz the top of the soap bar with rubbing alcohol once to prevent bubbles.

4 Allow the soap to harden for about an hour, then remove it from the mold.

Faux Flower Soap

Try making this soap with a luscious floral fragrance, then unwrap it in the dreary, gray dead of winter—February, say, when everything is covered with a layer of frost. The pretty flower and the warm scent will remind you that it will soon be time to shed those hats and boots, because spring is just around the corner.

YIELD: 1 BAR

Small faux flower
4–6 ounces clear soap base, cut into small cubes
Fragrance or essential oil (optional)
Deep-dish circular or dome-shaped soap mold
Spray bottle filled with rubbing alcohol

Remove any small parts of the flower, such as the stem, that are likely to break off or scratch the skin.

In a double boiler over low heat, or using the microwave at medium power, melt down the soap base, then remove it from the heat. If you'd like, add fragrance.

3 Set the melted soap aside and allow it to cool for a few minutes, until a thin skin forms on top. Your goal is to reach the correct temperature for floating the flower in the soap.

4 Pour the soap into the mold. Very gently press the flower upside down into the soap (so it'll be face up when you unmold the bar). Spritz the top of the bar with rubbing alcohol once to prevent bubbles.

5 Allow the soap to harden for about one hour, then carefully remove it from the mold.

Sassy
Soap

Sparkly Snow Dome Soap

This soap is a great showcase for your most unusual, treasured embedding-toy finds. Or, if you're a world traveler, maybe try creating a souvenir soap by embedding one of those refrigerator magnets you can find in gift shops around the globe.

YIELD: 1 BAR

3–4 ounces clear soap base,
cut into small cubes
Cosmetic-grade glitter
Dome-shaped soap mold
Small rubber or PVC toy of your choice
Spray bottle filled with rubbing alcohol
1 ounce white soap base,
cut into small cubes
Colorant of your choice

In a double boiler over low heat, or using the microwave at medium power, melt down the clear soap base, then remove it from the heat. Stir in a few pinches of cosmetic glitter.

Set the melted soap aside and allow it to cool for 5 minutes, until a thin skin forms on top. Your goal is to reach the correct temperature for floating the toy in the soap.

 Pour the clear glitter soap into the mold, carefully filling it about ¾ full. Gently drop the toy into the soap upside down (so it'll be face up when you unmold the bar). Spritz the top of the soap with rubbing alcohol once to prevent bubbles, and allow the soap to harden in the mold for approximately thirty minutes.

 Melt down the white soap base and add the colorant of your choice.

 Spritz the top of the soap in the mold once lightly. This will help the layers of soap to adhere to each other. Next, pour the opaque soap directly over the clear soap, filling the mold to the top.

Set the mold aside for about an hour before gently removing the soap.

NOTE: When choosing a colorant for the base of the dome, keep in mind that this project works best with slightly darker colors, such as grays, dark pinks, blues, reds, and greens. The purpose of a dark color is to create the illusion of depth under the rounded translucent layer—it will look a lot like a snow dome. (Not that you can't experiment with pastel colors for the base. You might achieve interesting effects.)

Sassy Soap

Spelling Bee Bar

This makes a happy back-to-school gift for kids, or a fun way to send a message to a friend. Arrange the colorful letters to spell a name, a message, or a secret code word. When they've used up the soap, they'll still have the letters to stick up on the fridge.

YIELD: 1 BAR

3 ounces clear soap base, cut into small cubes
Colorant of your choice
Fragrance or essential oil (optional)
Assorted small plastic letters
Plain soap mold
Spray bottle filled with rubbing alcohol

In a double boiler over low heat, or using the microwave at medium power, melt down the soap base, then remove it from the heat. Add the colorant of your choice and fragrance, if desired.

Set the melted soap aside and allow it to cool for a few minutes, until a thin skin forms on top. Your goal is to reach the correct temperature for floating the letters in the soap.

3 Pour the soap into the mold. Then, very gently, press the letters into the soap upside down (so they'll be face up when you unmold the bar), spelling a word if you like. Spritz the top of the bar with rubbing alcohol once to prevent bubbles.

4 Allow the soap to harden for about thirty minutes, then carefully remove it from the mold.

HINT: Small plastic letters are often available as magnets. So, not only can they work their magnetic magic on your body as you use the soap, but they can have a second life holding up the lovely artwork you post on your fridge! Look for them at a toy store or dollar shop.

Sassy
Soap

The Evil Eye Bar

This kooky, spooky eyeball soap is a great one to break out at Halloween time—or anytime you feel like the Mad Scientist in you simply must get out!

YIELD: 1 BAR

2–3 ounces white soap base, cut into small cubes
Oval soap mold
Plastic eyeball toy
Spray bottle filled with rubbing alcohol

 In a double boiler over low heat, or using the microwave at medium power, melt down the soap base, then remove it from the heat and set it aside to cool slightly.

 Gently pour the soap base into the mold, filling it about ¾ full. Spritz the bottom of the eye lightly with rubbing alcohol, then carefully place it in the soap, leaving about half of the eye above the surface. It may be necessary to hold the toy down for a few minutes as the soap hardens around it. If any tiny bubbles appear, get rid of them with a quick spritzing of rubbing alcohol.

Allow the soap to cool for about thirty minutes before carefully removing it from the mold.

Sassy Soap

Squiggles and Swirls Soap

With its colorful shreds embedded in a translucent base, this bar is like a festive handful of confetti—a miniature tickertape parade encapsulated in soap! Keep it at home to lift your spirits when you hop in the shower. It also makes a great "Congratulations!" gift for a buddy.

YIELD: 1 BAR

2 ounces white soap base, cut into small cubes and then divided into three or four equal portions
3–4 shades of colorant (colors of your choice)
3–4 shallow plastic food storage containers
Kitchen tool such as a potato peeler or paring knife
Soap mold in the shape of your choice
2–3 ounces clear soap base, cut into small cubes
Fragrance or essential oil (optional)
Spray bottle filled with rubbing alcohol

 In a double boiler over low heat, or using the microwave at medium power, melt down a portion of the white soap base, then remove it from the heat, stir in one of the colorants, and set the soap aside to cool slightly.

65

 Pour the colored mixture into a shallow plastic food storage container and allow it to harden.

 Repeat the same process with the remaining two or three batches of white soap base and the remaining shades of colorant.

 Allow the colored soap to harden for about 10 minutes before gently removing them from the containers.

 Use the potato peeler or paring knife to make squiggly shapes out of the colored soaps. Place these pieces in a random pattern in the soap mold.

 Melt down the clear soap base and add in fragrance, if desired. Then set it aside to cool until a thin skin forms over the top. It is especially important to let the clear soap cool as much as possible because, if it is too hot, it may melt the soap shapes in the mold.

Sassy
Soap

 Spritz rubbing alcohol on the soap pieces in the mold. Then pour the clear soap over them (try not to pour directly onto the colored soap). Allow the bar to harden for about 40 minutes before removing it from the mold.

VARIATION:

 You're not restricted to the vegetable peeler here. A melon baller, mini cookie cutters, or any other utensils you may have around will produce terrific shapes for embedding.

"How wonderfully they make this soap," he said, gazing at a piece of soap he was handling, which Agafea Mihalovna had put ready for the visitor but Oblonsky had not used. "Only look; why, it's a work of art."

"Yes, everything's brought to such a pitch of perfection nowadays," said Stepan Arkadyevich, with a moist and blissful yawn.

—Konstantin Levin to Prince Stepan Arkadyevich Oblonsky, in Leo Tolstoy's *Anna Karenina*, 1878

Sassy Soap

Citrus Wedge Soap

So many things are better with a wedge of citrus floating in them, aren't they? Iced tea, sparkling water, a bowl of punch. . . So isn't it only reasonable to decide that a simple bar of soap would benefit from having the same garnish?

YIELD: 2 BARS

6–8 ounces clear soap base,
cut into small cubes and divided
into three equal portions
Orange colorant
1 ounce white soap base,
cut into small cubes
Small round soap mold
Larger rectangular mold
Fragrance or essential oil (optional)

 In a double boiler over low heat, or using the microwave at medium power, melt down a portion of the clear soap base. Stir in a drop of colorant, then pour the soap into the small round mold and set it aside to cool.

 When soap has hardened, carefully remove it from the mold and cut it into three to six small triangular wedges. Pare a little bit of soap—about an $1/8$ inch—off the edges of each wedge, and put the wedges back into the round mold. They should fit quite loosely, with some space between them.

69

Melt down the white soap and allow it to cool for a few minutes before drizzling it slowly into the mold to fill the space surrounding the translucent wedges. Once the soap has hardened, remove it from the mold. Cut it down the center to make two slices of fruit.

Melt down the second portion of clear soap base and allow it to cool slightly, then pour it into the rectangular mold. After it has cooled for a few minutes longer and developed a thin skin around the top, carefully drop a citrus wedge into the clear soap. Allow the bar to cool completely before removing it from the mold.

Repeat step 4 with the remaining clear soap base to make the second bar.

VARIATIONS:

 You can, of course, make any sort of citrus fruit by varying your choice of colorant. Try yellow for lemon, green for lime, and pink for grapefruit.

 If you prefer, instead of embedding the citrus wedges in soap bars, you can use them alone as hand soaps.

Sassy
Soap

Heading into Deeper Waters: Loaf Soaps

Loaf soaps are a great way to make several bars at a time without having to keep

refilling molds. You fill one large mold, then slice it into a whole bunch of identical bars.

And, by cleverly assembling the elements of the loaf, you can create fabulous designs

in the soap. Cook up a loaf next time you need a batch of gifts.

A Piece of My Heart
Soap Loaf

This soap is a natural for Valentine's Day, of course. But, really, when is it ever inappropriate to give a gift that expresses your heartfelt good wishes?

YIELD: 4–6 BARS

Premade heart-shaped soap log
(available in stores)
Pink colorant
Fragrance or essential oil (optional)
1–1$\frac{1}{2}$ pounds white soap base,
cut into small cubes (amount depends
on the size of the loaf mold)
Loaf mold

In a double boiler over low heat, or using the microwave at medium power, melt down the soap base, stir in one or two drops of colorant, and add fragrance if desired. Remove the soap from the heat and set it aside to cool for three to five minutes.

Sassy
Soap

 Meanwhile, cut the heart-shaped log to fit the loaf mold and place the log into the mold in a manner that appeals to you. If you are using small heart logs, you may choose to put two in the mold, as shown in the photograph.

 When the soap base is as cool as possible—but still pourable—drizzle it slowly into the mold, filling the mold to the top. Take care not to pour it directly onto the heart logs, or they will melt and lose their shape.

 Allow the soap to harden for several hours before carefully pressing on the mold to release the loaf.

 Using a sharp knife, cut the loaf into individual bars. Each will have the heart-shaped design.

Festive Fruitcake Soap Loaf

True, real fruitcakes are the joke of the holiday season. But these colorful, confetti-like bars are sure to be appreciated—at Christmas or any other time. Not to mention they make a great way to use up all those teeny scraps of colorful soap you have left over from other projects.

YIELD: 4–6 BARS

1–1½ pounds white soap base, cut into small cubes (amount depends on the size of the loaf mold)
5–8 ounces mixed, colored soap, cut into chunks
Loaf mold
Spray bottle filled with rubbing alcohol
Fragrance or essential oil (optional)

1 Jumble (or neatly arrange, if you prefer) the soap chunks into the loaf mold and spritz them lightly with rubbing alcohol.

2 In a double boiler over low heat, or using the microwave at medium power, melt down the white soap base, then remove it from the heat and add fragrance, if desired. Set the soap aside to cool for three to five minutes.

Sassy Soap

When the soap base is as cool as possible, but still pourable, drizzle it slowly into the mold, filling the mold to the top. Try to avoid pouring it directly onto the soap chunks.

Allow the soap to harden for several hours before carefully pressing on the mold to release the loaf.

Using a sharp knife, cut the loaf into individual bars. Alternatively, try using a crinkle cutter (available at any kitchen supply shop) to give the bars a more unusual appearance.

NOTE: I used clear, colored soap scraps for this project, but you can use opaque ones too. Or a mixture. If you don't have any scraps, just melt down some soap base, add colorant, and pour the soap into small, standard-sized molds. Once the soap is cool, unmold it and chop it into whatever size chunks you like.

Ancient Papyrus Scroll Soap

This beautiful, rustic soap cylinder looks like an ancient artifact—maybe from a pharaoh's tomb. It makes fantastic hand soap.

YIELD: 2–3 BARS

5 ounces clear soap base, cut into small cubes
1 ounce or less white soap base
Crushed lavender or other additive
Small plastic cutting board, preferably textured
Pan large enough to hold the cutting board

1 In a double boiler over low heat, or using the microwave at medium power, melt down the clear soap base, and add just a touch of white soap. Your goal is just to give the base a milky, semi-opaque look. Stir in the lavender or other additive. Remove the soap from the heat and add fragrance, if desired. Set the soap aside to cool slightly.

2 Place the cutting board into the pan to catch any drips and spills, then carefully pour the soap blend onto the cutting board to form a thin layer. Allow that layer to harden and dry. This will not take long—probably about ten minutes. When the soap is cool to the touch, gently peel it off the cutting board.

"I tell you, it's easy to clean up here. Hot and cold water on tap, just as much as you like, there is. Woolly towels, there is; and a towel horse so hot, it burns your fingers. Soft brushes to scrub yourself, and a wooden bowl of soap smelling like primroses. Now I know why ladies is so clean. Washing's a treat for them."

—Liza Doolittle, in George Bernard Shaw's Pygmalion, 1916

 Roll the soap up into a scroll.

NOTE: I used crushed lavender for this soap, but you have an almost endless choice of alternatives. Try calendula flower petals, ground oatmeal, or poppy seeds.

Loofah Loaf-ah Bar

This is a great project for so many reasons. It's economical: All it takes is one loofah to make several bars of soap. It's useful: Loofah sponges are well known for their gentle exfoliating properties. And it's lovely: The loofah makes a nice lacy pattern in the translucent bar.

YIELD: 4–6 BARS

1–1$\frac{1}{2}$ pounds clear soap base, cut into small cubes
Colorant
Fragrance or essential oil (optional)
Loofah sponge
Loaf mold

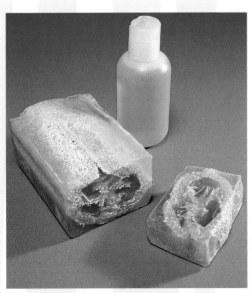

In a double boiler over low heat, or using the microwave at medium power, melt down the clear soap base, then remove it from the heat and add one or two drops of colorant and fragrance, if desired. Set the soap aside to cool slightly.

SOAP LORE: It is a tradition among **Welsh** washerwomen to say that new work is coming whenever a bar of soap falls on the floor.

 Place the loofah sponge into the loaf mold, then pour the melted soap over it until the entire thing is fully coated and submerged. The loofah may float up a bit—if it does, simply push it down with a spoon or other implement and hold it until enough soap soaks into it for it to sink.

 Allow the soap to harden for several hours before carefully pressing on the mold to release the loaf.

 Using a sharp knife, cut the loaf into individual bars.

Cheeky Checkerboard Soap Loaf

This perky bar, with its chunks of vivid color, will brighten anyone's outlook. This is the bar you want to encounter in your shower early on a Monday morning, when you're wishing like anything that the weekend wasn't over.

YIELD: 4–6 BARS

3–4 different colors of precolored
opaque soap base
(each approximately ¹/₄ pound)
8–14 ounces clear soap base,
depending on the size
of the loaf mold
Loaf mold
Fragrance or essential oil
(optional)

Using a sharp knife, cut the colored soap base into lengthwise strips that will fit into your loaf mold. Spritz the strips lightly with rubbing alcohol and stack them so that they'll form a checkerboard pattern when you cut the loaf into bars.

In a double boiler over low heat, or using the microwave at medium power, melt down the clear soap base, then remove it from the heat and add fragrance, if desired. Set the soap aside to cool for three to five minutes.

When the soap base is as cool as possible, but still pourable, drizzle it slowly into the mold, filling the mold to the top.

Allow the soap to harden for several hours before carefully pressing on the mold to release the loaf.

Using a sharp knife, cut the loaf into individual bars.

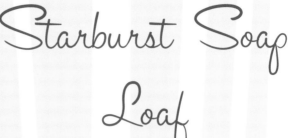

Starburst Soap Loaf

Think of this as the soap equivalent of Fourth of July fireworks, with the colorful stars bursting out of each bar.

Tube molds like the star molds called for here aren't usually difficult to find. Check at kitchen supply stores—some craft shops carry them, too. The molds, originally intended to make shaped bread for fancy little canapé sandwiches, are fairly inexpensive and will last a long time if they are well cared for.

YIELD: 4–6 BARS

Star-shaped tube mold
8–14 ounces white soap base, cut into small cubes
Fragrance or essential oil (optional)
Red and blue colorant
1–1½ pounds clear soap base, cut into small cubes
Loaf pan

In a double boiler over low heat, or using the microwave at medium power, melt down the white soap base, then remove it from the heat and add fragrance, if desired. Set the soap aside to cool slightly.

Sassy Soap

2 Make sure that the cap at the end of the star-shaped mold is on tightly, then pour the melted soap into the mold. Let the soap harden for about an hour, then remove the cap from the end of the mold and gently push to release the soap.

3 Cut the star soap to the length of the loaf pan and place it in the pan.

4 Repeat steps 1 through 3 twice more, this time adding the red and then the blue colorants before pouring the soap into the star mold.

5 When all the star soaps have been placed in the loaf pan, melt down the clear soap and add fragrance, if desired. Let the melted soap base sit for three to five minutes. When it is

as cool as possible, but still pourable, drizzle it slowly into a corner of the mold (not directly onto the star soap), filling the mold to the top. Allow part of a star soap to stick out the top, if desired.

6 Allow the soap to harden for several hours before carefully pressing on the mold to release the loaf.

5 Using a sharp knife, cut the loaf into individual bars.

VARIATION:

 Make a Starry Night soap by using dark blue colorant for the background color. Use clear soap with cosmetic glitter in it to make the star shapes. You may also be able to find a moon-shaped tube mold so you can add a moon to the loaf.

Sassy Soap

C H A P T E R   6

Fancy Moves:
Unique and Novelty Projects

As you've probably gathered by now, one of the great things about working with melt-and-pour soap is the sheer versatility of it. Not only can it be made into bars, but you can also add toys and create clever soap-within-soap designs. In this chapter you'll learn how to make unique soaps, from the fashionable to the funky—and always, of course, functional.

Many of these projects involve working with novelty candy or chocolate molds, which usually aren't intended to handle the high temperatures that melt-and-pour soapmaking entails. The best solution is to make a rubber latex copy of the mold (see pages 19–21 for instructions). You'll be able to use it hundreds of times—and if you're still not tired of the mold when the latex wears out, you can go back to the original mold to cast a new one.

Since the size of the mold you use could be quite a bit different from the size of the ones I've got, I don't include the amounts of soap base needed for the projects in this chapter. But by now you're getting to be an old hand at this soapmaking thing! Just fill your mold with water and pour that into a measuring cup to figure out how much base you need.

Sassy Soap

Sudsy Cell Phone Bar

We all know them—those people who never go anywhere without their cell phones attached to their ears. Now you can give 'em a phone to hang on to even in the shower! Go for strictly realistic gray or try out wild candy-apple red to make a crazier conversation piece. A touch of glitter gives this bar just the right glitzy shimmer.

YIELD: 1 BAR

White or clear soap base,
cut into small cubes
Colorant of your choice
Cosmetic-grade glitter
or silver mica
Fragrance or essential oil (optional)
Cell phone chocolate mold, or a latex mold
(see pages 19–21 for instructions)

 In a double boiler over low heat, or using the microwave at medium power, melt down the soap base, then remove it from the heat. Add the colorant and a pinch of glitter or mica, then stir in fragrance, if desired.

 Pour the soap into the mold and allow it to harden before gently removing the bar.

NOTE: I found this mold at a chocolate shop. If there isn't a candy supply store in your area, check out mail-order catalogs or chocolate-making supply websites. You could probably also make a nice latex mold from one of those children's toys shaped like a phone.

Sassy
Soap

Bubblicious Box o' Chocs Soaps

These delectable little beauties make a great gift, especially when they're presented complete with ruffly paper wrappers in a pretty bonbon box (you can get inexpensive boxes at most party supply stores). You might also want to enhance the illusion by blending in a sweet fragrance like chocolate, amaretto, or vanilla. Be sure to mark them clearly as soap—these little sweeties look like real sweets!

YIELD: ASSORTED SMALL HAND-SOAP-SIZED BARS

White soap base,
cut into small cubes
Brown or tan colorant
Bonbon-shaped molds or
latex molds (see pages
19–21 for instructions)
Fragrance or essential oil
(optional)
Spray bottle filled with
rubbing alcohol (optional)
Potato peeler (optional)

1   In a double boiler over low heat, or using the microwave at medium power, melt down the soap base, then remove it from the heat. Add the colorant and stir in fragrance, if desired.

2   Pour the mix into the decorative candy molds and allow them to cool before carefully unmolding them.

3   To spruce your bonbons up even more, add toppings. Place the soaps on a piece of wax paper and spritz them lightly with alcohol. Melt some additional white soap base, tint it with colorant if desired, and lightly drizzle it over the bonbons in a zigzag motion. Or, if you'd like, use a potato peeler and a solid piece of white soap base to scrape little "coconut" shreds over the tops.

Sassy
Soap

Gothic Coffin Bar

Looking for an eerie party favor for your Halloween haunted house party? Your search is over. This great 3-D mold came from a chocolate-making supply shop in New England, but can also be found in mail-order catalogs and on candy supply websites. There are three separate pieces: the coffin, the skeleton, and the lid. By using different colors and shades you can create a sense of depth.

YIELD: 1 BAR

White soap base, cut into small cubes
Clear soap base, cut into small cubes
Coffin-shaped candy mold or latex mold (see pages 19–21 for instructions)
Gray colorant, or red and blue food coloring
Fragrance or essential oil (optional)
Spray bottle filled with rubbing alcohol

In a double boiler over low heat, or using the microwave at medium power, melt down a small amount of the white soap base, then remove it from the heat and allow it to cool slightly. Pour the soap into the skeleton section of the mold. Allow this section to cool, then spritz the surface lightly with alcohol.

91

 Melt down more of the white soap base, add in gray colorant (or use one drop blue and one drop red food coloring to create a similar hue), and allow it to cool slightly. Pour it into the lower portion of the coffin mold.

 Melt down the clear soap base and pour it into the lid portion of the mold.

 When all of the sections have hardened, gently remove the soap pieces from their molds and fit them all together.

Sassy
Soap

Yer Under Arrest! Handcuffs Bar

This novelty bar will capture their interest! For the most realistic look, use gray colorant, or combine one drop blue and one drop red food coloring to create a similar hue. Or make 'em crazy colors for an extra arresting (wink, wink) look.

YIELD: 1 BAR

White soap base, cut into small cubes
Colorant of your choice
Cosmetic-grade glitter or silver mica
Fragrance or essential oil (optional)
Handcuff-shaped chocolate mold
or latex mold (see pages 19–21 for
instructions)

 In a double boiler over low heat, or using the microwave at medium power, melt down the soap base, then remove it from the heat.

 Add the colorant and stir in the glitter to give the cuffs a nice metallic shimmer. Add fragrance, if desired.

 Gently pour the soap into the mold and allow it to sit until hardened.

Soapy Sushi Squares

This is your chance to test out your skills as a sushi chef. (Technically, by the way, this isn't a melt-and-pour soap project—you don't do any melting. But the results are pretty terrific.) These little faux sushi rolls make great hand soaps for anyone, but will especially suit the sushi fiend in your life.

YIELD: VARIES, DEPENDING ON THE SIZE OF THE BARS

White soap base
Small scraps orange and green soap
Round pen or narrow paintbrush
Round or square mini cookie cutters (optional)

 Using a sharp knife, cut several cubes from a brick of white soap base. If you're going for an authentic sushi look, make them hand-soap size (1 to 1½ inches). For a bath-sized bar, cut a three-inch square.

Cut several small, rectangular strips off the colored soaps. These will serve as cucumbers and carrot slivers.

Carefully poke a hole in the top center of each cube using the back of a pen or narrow paintbrush. Insert the soap cucumbers and carrots and press very gently on the white portion of the soap to push the veggies into the "rice" cube so they don't fall out.

NOTE: These soaps look great presented in a plastic sushi tray or arranged on a matte-finish pottery dish.

Flower-Power Soap Pops

Move over, Marsha Brady. This groovy soap on a stick is great for that friend with a penchant for the '70s, or simply as a fun replacement for bringing flowers to a host. They look particularly good displayed in mini clay pots. Make them in bright colors and take a bouquet!

YIELD: 2 BARS

Flower-shaped soap mold
Small circular cookie cutter
Shallow pan
Clear soap base, cut into small cubes
2 shades of colorant (colors of your choice)
2 popsicle sticks

 In a double boiler over low heat, or using the microwave at medium power, melt down half of the soap base and add the colorant of your choice.

 Pour the soap into the flower mold and set it aside. Once the soap has hardened, carefully remove it from the mold and use the cookie cutter to make a hole through the center.

Sassy Soap

Repeat steps 1 and 2 with the remaining soap base, tinting it a different color.

Place a circle in the center of the flower of the opposite color and carefully push the popsicle stick into the flower. Repeat this step, placing the other circle into the center of the remaining flower and inserting the stick.

Medicine Bottle Bar

This funny little hand-soap sized bar is just what the doctor ordered when you want to cheer up a friend who's under the weather. Works great as a gift for a recent med-school graduate, too.

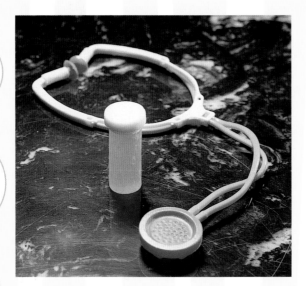

YIELD: 1 BAR

White soap base, cut into small cubes
Latex mold of a plastic prescription bottle (see pages 19–21 for instructions)
Clear soap base, cut into small cubes
Orange colorant
Stick-on faux prescription label (optional)

 In a double boiler over low heat, or using the microwave at medium power, melt down a small amount of white soap base, then pour it into the cap portion of the mold. Allow the soap to harden for approximately twenty minutes, or until it forms a thick skin.

Sassy Soap

SOAP LORE: It might surprise you to learn that although soap was probably known in ancient Rome—home of those famously decadent baths—it wasn't used for bathing. When Romans bathed, they rubbed themselves with olive oil, then scraped their bodies clean with a metal device called a strigil.

 Melt down the clear soap and stir in a few drops of orange colorant. Pour the soap into the mold, filling it almost to the top. Set it aside and allow it to harden for an hour to an hour and a half.

 Removing the soap can be a bit tricky. It is best accomplished by gently peeling back the mold until the soap is released. If you're going for a really authentic look, print up a faux prescription label on your computer.

"You may seek it with thimbles—and seek it with care;
You may hunt it with forks and hope;
You may threaten its life with a railway-share;
You may charm it with smiles and soap—"

("That's exactly the method," the Bellman bold
In a hasty parenthesis cried,
"That's exactly the way I have always been told
That the capture of Snarks should be tried!")

—Lewis Carroll, from *The Hunting of the Snark*, 1876

Tattoo You Bar

Suppose you've made a very nice but rather plain bar of soap and you're suddenly in the mood to jazz it up. There's a quick way—temporary tattoos. With such a wide selection available, from exotic mendhi patterns to cute cartoon characters, you're bound to find something that suits your mood.

Keep in mind that this is a temporary solution, though. The design will start to disintegrate and wear away after a few hand washings.

YIELD: 1 BAR

Finished bar of soap
Temporary tattoo

Wet the back of the temporary tattoo and place it face down on the top of the bar of soap. Rub the tattoo's paper backing lightly for about twenty seconds, then carefully peel the paper away. The tattoo will be safely transferred to the soap bar.

Wedding Cake Soap Set

Tint these soaps with the bride's choice of colors for that special day—they'll make fantastic party favors. Cake toppers are available at party stores and wedding supply shops. If you prefer the vintage look—and there are lots of great brides and grooms out there from decades past—visit flea markets and online auctions.

YIELD: 3 VARIOUSLY SIZED BARS

White soap base,
cut into small cubes
Colorant of your choice
Shallow pan
3 round cookie cutters,
in varying sizes
Plastic wedding-cake couple

1. In a double boiler over low heat, or using the microwave at medium power, melt down enough white soap base to fill the shallow pan to a level of about an inch. Stir in the colorant of your choice.

 Pour the soap into the shallow pan and set it aside until it has hardened completely. Turn the soap out onto a flat surface and use the cookie cutters to stamp out a small, a medium, and a large circle.

 Stack the soap circles like a tiered wedding cake, with the largest on the bottom and the smallest on top. Place the bride and groom cake topper on the soap.

VARIATIONS:

 Adapt this tiered soap for any occasion: Simply use a birthday cake topper or other decoration instead of the bride and groom.

 You don't have to stick with round cookie cutters; try using square or star-shaped cookie cutters, too.

Pop-Together Op-Art Circle Bars

This project makes three separate bars of soap that are similar in appearance but have different color patterns. Using the cookie cutters, you cut out the pieces, mix 'em up a bit, and pop them back together again. It's a snap!

YIELD: 3 HAND-SOAP SIZE BARS

3 round cookie cutters in varying sizes
Clear soap base, cut into small cubes and divided into three equal batches
3 shades of colorants (colors of your choice)
3 mixing bowls
3 flexible, shallow pans or molds

In a double boiler over low heat, or using the microwave at medium power, melt down a batch of the clear soap base, then add the colorant of your choice. Pour it into a shallow pan or mold. You want the layer of soap to be fairly thin, between a quarter and a half inch deep.

Repeat this process with the other two batches of soap, tinting each a different color and pouring it into its own pan. Set the pans aside for thirty to forty minutes, or until the soap has solidified.

Sassy Soap

Once all three colors of soap have hardened, remove them from their respective pans and stack them on top of each other like a sandwich.

Using the largest cookie cutter, cut through the soap sandwich. You'll then have three large circles stacked on top of each other. Carefully remove them from the cookie cutter.

Using the medium-sized cookie cutter, cut a hole through the large-circle sandwich. There's no need to center the hole in the circle (unless you prefer to). Off-center will work very well. Remove that soap sandwich and repeat the process using the smallest cookie cutter.

Gently separate all the soap pieces, then place different-colored ones inside of each as if you're putting a jigsaw puzzle together. Press the pieces together firmly so that they adhere to one another.

Lucky Dice Soap

No need to worry that you're encouraging a friend's gambling habit when you give a pair of these as a gift. With these dice, you always clean up!

YIELD: 2 BARS

White soap base, cut into small cubes
and separated into two equal batches
Square three-dimensional soap mold
1–2 blank stick-on labels
Black magic marker
Hole punch
Plastic wrap

Soap Lore: According to legend, the notorious bank robber, John Dillinger, was a talented soap carver. He is said to have whittled a bar of soap into the shape of a gun, stained it with black shoe polish, and used it to break out of the Crown Point, Indiana, jail in 1934. A few months later, though, he was killed in a shoot-out at the Biograph Theater in Chicago.

 In a double boiler over low heat, or using the microwave at medium power, melt down a batch of the white soap base and pour it into the mold. Allow it to harden and then remove it. Wrap the soap in plastic wrap.

 Repeat this process for the second bar.

 Color the labels with the black magic marker and, once the ink has dried, use the hole punch to cut out forty-two dots. Remove the dots from their paper backing and stick them onto the sides of the wrapped soaps to make the bars look like dice.

Shimmering Rock Crystal Bar

With a little ingenuity, almost anything can be inspiration for a soapmaking project, such as a beautiful amethyst at a museum gift shop. For this project, I used a geode to make a mold. (Some people believe that rock crystals have healing powers. That may or may not be—but a rock crystal bar of soap is definitely soothing.)

YIELD: 1 BAR

Latex mold of a geode or other medium-sized crystalline rock (see pages 19–21 for instructions)
Clear soap base, cut into small cubes
Colorant of your choice
Fragrance or essential oil (optional)
Cosmetic-grade glitter

 In a double boiler over low heat, or using the microwave at medium power, melt down the clear soap base, then add the colorant of your choice and fragrance, if desired.

 Pour the soap into the mold and allow it to harden for about thirty minutes.

 Carefully remove the soap from the mold and sprinkle a few pinches of cosmetic glitter over the top to create a realistic, sparkly appearance.

Summer Berry Soaps

They smell just like strawberries. They look just like strawberries. Great for the berry lover in your midst, these festive little soaps would make terrific guest soaps at a summerhouse. Pack 'em in a simple plastic strawberry basket with some raffia and you're good to go.

YIELD: ASSORTED SMALL HAND SOAPS

White soap base, cut into small cubes
Red colorant
Fragrance or essential oil (optional)
Rubber ice cube tray shaped like strawberries or other fruit
Spray bottle filled with rubbing alcohol

Sassy Soap

1. In a double boiler over low heat, or using the microwave at medium power, melt down the soap base, add the colorant, and stir in the fragrance, if desired.

2. Carefully pour the soap into the cavities of the ice cube tray mold. If any tiny air bubbles surface, spritz the soap with a touch of rubbing alcohol.

3. Set the soap aside to harden for thirty to forty minutes before gently removing the soaps from the mold.

"When I pick up
a bar
of soap
to take a closer look,
its powerful aroma
astounds me:
O fragrance,
I don't know
Where you come from,
—what
is your home town?..."

Pablo Neruda,
"Ode to a bar of soap"

Floating Flower Soap

Use your colorful scraps from other projects to make these pretty little posies floating in a translucent base. This soap has a fun look that's sweet but contemporary. It's great fun to make and use.

YIELD: 1 BAR

Colorful scraps of soap in the colors of your choice
Small, shallow plastic container
Tiny flower-shaped cookie cutters or small floral-motif craft molds
Clear soap base, cut into small cubes
Fragrance or essential oil (optional)
Rectangular or square soap mold
Toothpick (if needed)
Spray bottle filled with rubbing alcohol

 In a double boiler over low heat or using the microwave at medium power, melt down one of the colored soap scraps and pour it into a small container to harden. Repeat this step with the other colors of soap scraps.

 Using the cutters, cut out pieces to make a floral design. Decide how the pieces will be arranged in the soap and set them aside.

Sassy Soap

Melt down the clear soap base, add fragrance if desired, set it aside to cool slightly, then fill the mold almost to the top. Watch for a skin to form on the soap base as it starts to harden.

Once the skin has begun to form on the soap, gently drop or press the pieces of the flower into place. If necessary, use a toothpick to nudge them into position. If you notice air bubbles forming, spritz a bit of rubbing alcohol on the surface of the soap.

5 Allow the soap to harden in the mold for about forty minutes before removing it.

VARIATIONS:

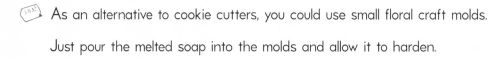
As an alternative to cookie cutters, you could use small floral craft molds. Just pour the melted soap into the molds and allow it to harden.

For complete control of how the flowers come out, turn sculptor! Melt down the soap, pour it into the tray, and then use a knife to cut out freeform floral shapes.

Sassy
Soap

The Soap Soap Box

Box molds are fairly commonly sold as candy molds and as plaster-casting molds. They are certainly an interesting choice for melt-and-pour soap projects, especially when you're giving them as a gift. Fill the box with bath beads, bath salts, toys, or other little soaps—and when the goodies are gone, the box itself can do its job as a bar of soap!

YIELD: 1 TWO-PART BAR

Clear or white soap base
Colorant (optional)
Fragrance or essential oil (optional)
Box-type mold

1. It is very important that the mold be level when you pour the melted soap into it. You may need to put a book or wooden block against a portion of the mold to hold it upright so that the soap doesn't spill all over the place.

2. In a double boiler over low heat or using the microwave at medium power, melt down the soap base. Add in colorant and fragrance if desired, then set the soap aside to cool slightly.

3. Slowly pour the melted soap into the box mold and allow it to harden for about 1 hour before carefully removing it.

Sassy Soap

Wrapping It Up!: Now That the Soap's Out of the Mold

Finishing Touches

So now you've made your soap, and it looks terrific. The first thing you need to do is wrap it in plastic or cellophane. Melt-and-pour soap will dry out unless it's wrapped. And . . . don't you want to create a package that will do your handiwork justice? Especially if you're going to give it to someone as a gift, rather than just stash it under your sink until you need it.

Here are a few ways to make fun labels at home that will really make your soap projects shine.

A FEW REMINDERS:

Melt-and-pour soap must be wrapped to prevent moisture loss. Cellophane works well (you'll find little cellophane bags at party supply stores), but plastic wrap is even better.

If you've used additives or fragrances, say so on the label. Many people have allergies and sensitive skin.

If the soap has a toy inside, especially if it is small enough to pose a choking hazard, label the soap as being "for ages three and up."

LABELING YOUR SOAP

It's easy and fun. Just take a picture (keep in mind that a bar of soap is usually just three or four inches wide, so the images should be small; if the original is too big, reduce it on a photocopier or scanner), type or write out any text you want to include, arrange the picture on the label the way you want it, and use rubber cement or double-sided tape to attach the makeshift label to a piece of paper so you can copy it. Alternatively, you can scan the image, use a graphics program to make labels, and print them out.

Attach the label to the soap using a piece of clear packaging tape that's slightly larger than the label. Or, for a more professional appearance, use adhesive paper rather than regular paper when you photocopy or print out the labels (you'll probably need to do this at a copy shop).

WHERE TO LOOK FOR LABEL ART

magazines

newspapers

comic books

wrapping paper

your own or a child's drawings

clip art (collections of free or inexpensive images available on CD-ROM)

Then you can just peel off the backing and stick the label on.

You can also make great one-of-a-kind labels by writing directly onto a blank label or decorative piece of paper. I'm partial to using the colorful yet muted dual-tone pages of Japanese comic books for this. Rubber stamps are another fun way to decorate blank labels.

OTHER PACKAGING IDEAS

Wicker baskets are lovely and traditional. Why reinvent the wheel? For a vintage twist on a basket, scour your attic or secondhand stores for a terrific hat. Flip it upside down, line it with tissue paper, and arrange the soaps inside. Wrap the whole thing up in cellophane or inexpensive tulle.

Play up the theme. Food-shaped soaps look great in take-out containers. Or, say you've made a frog soap. Cut out an oval piece of cardboard and wrap it in a green washcloth to make it look like a lily pad. Set the soap on top, put everything in a large cellophane bag, and glue small plastic flies to the cellophane with a hot glue gun.

Those little cardboard boxes that jewelry comes in are perfect for holding travel- or sample-sized bars. Paint the box, découpage it, or decorate it with rhinestones.

Clear plastic boxes make great displays for three-dimensional soaps. Line the bottom with something eye-catching, like iridescent plastic shreds (the kind you find in Easter baskets) or colorful foil.

Explore the hardware store to get great ideas for packaging with an industrial look. I once made a soap dish by gluing together a few pieces of narrow PVC pipe.

Of course, if you're still in a crafty mood after making the soap, you might consider whipping up a soap dish to store it in, too . . .

SOAP LORE: On March 15, 2003, a group of volunteers gathered to create the world's largest bar of soap. The product of their efforts eventually weighed in at more than eight tons—about twice as much as the previous Guinness Book of World Records title-holder. It took 130 pounds of fragrance to give the blue-tinted bar just the right scent. Afterward, the bar was cut up into more than 65,000 normal-sized bars to be sold and distributed to charities. The project was part of a fund-raising effort to support research into the skin disease scleroderma.

Sassy
Soap

Problem-Solving, Questions and Answers

Questions? Problems? Here are answers to some of the concerns that may arise.

Q: **My clear melt-and-pour soap base isn't totally clear. In fact, it's kind of yellowish. What gives?**

A: Most clear melt-and-pour base will have a yellowish tint. It's nothing to be concerned about. Many manufacturers add alcohol to the soap to help maintain a perfectly clear appearance—the higher the alcohol content, the more transparent the soap is. While that may be more visually appealing, though, it dries the skin more.

Q: **My soap has white blotches that look like a rash. What's that?**

A: This problem is caused by poor quality soap base. Try using a different brand or manufacturer.

Q: I know I should use cosmetic-grade scents. Well, my favorite perfume smells great, and it's obviously cosmetic-grade. Can I use it in my soap?

A: You can, but it's not an ideal means of scenting soap. Most perfumes have a high alcohol content, which means that the scent will fade much faster than fragrance or essential oils.

Q: Can I mix clear melt-and-pour soap base with the opaque variety?

A: Absolutely. You'll get a semitranslucent look.

"They tell me there's some people in this world takes a bath every week!"

—Maxwell Anderson, from *All Quiet on the Western Front*, 1930

Q: My soap project came out so ugly it would scare small children. Is it salvageable?

A: This is the beauty of melt-and-pour soap! Melt it down and try again. (And hope that all the colors combine into something attractive!) Melt-and-pour soap base has

Sassy Soap

a high moisture content, so if you repeatedly rebatch the same soap base, the end product will eventually get waxy or flaky. But remelting a failed project once or twice shouldn't cause that problem.

Q: **How should I store my soapmaking supplies? Also, what is the shelflife of my finished soap projects?**

A: Soap base, fragrance oils, and additives should be stored in a cool, dry place. They should be useable for at least two to three years, if not longer. Of course, as time goes on fragrance oils may start to lose their staying power. As far as finished soaps go, that will depend on their environment and exposure to the elements. It's been my experience that melt-and-pour soaps are at their best when used within a year to a year and a half.

Q: **I'm thinking about going into business selling my soaps. What should I know and how much should I charge per bar?**

A: Pricing will vary depending on your location and the demand for handmade products. Tally up your cost per bar, taking into account what you paid for the soap base, colorant, additives, the molds, and fragrances. A general rule of thumb is that the retail price should be at least $1.00 to $1.50 per ounce.

There are many markets for handmade soap, including high-end boutiques, craft fairs, malls, and home parties. Think about alternative means of marketing your product, too, such as selling your soaps as favors for special events or making corporate gift baskets for the holidays.

Packaging need not be ornate, but it should be professional looking. The labels should include an ingredient list and information on how your company can be contacted (i.e., website address and phone number).

When you're just getting started, it makes sense to handle sales and marketing yourself. As your business grows, there's always the possibility of hiring sales reps in various parts of the country to make contact with larger-scale retailers.

Before you decide to sell your creations, though, be sure to check with local government agencies to determine whether any business licenses are required. Also, consider purchasing liability insurance. It's quite inexpensive and an important asset in protecting your business.

Sassy
Soap

Index

Sassy
Soap

Acknowledgments

Many thanks to editors Danielle Truscott and Ana Deboo,
designer Kay Shuckhart, and photographer Michael Hnatov for all of their
hard work in making this book come together.

About the Author

Faith Sugarman is a freelance writer and craftsperson who hails from the New York City area. Her articles and crafts reviews have been featured in various print and online publications.

In 1998 she began selling her unique melt-and-pour soap creations online, as well as maintaining a creative-living website that features myriad topics including kitschy crafts, cool collections, and gardening. She now resides in New England with her eight-pound Wonderdog and her snuggly, lovable cat, and is working on additional crafts books and projects.